PUBERTY

Susan Elliot-Wright

Raintree

Chicago, Illinois

Design: Carole Binding
Photo research: Glass Onion Pictures

Printed in Hong Kong by Wing King Tong.

1 2 3 4 5 6 7 8 9 0
07 06 05 04 03

Library of Congress Cataloging-in-Publication Data:

Elliot-Wright, Susan.
  Puberty / Susan Elliot-Wright.
    v. cm. -- (Health issues)
  Includes bibliographical references and index.
  Contents: What is puberty? -- Physical changes -- Looking after yourself -- A changing body, changing feelings -- Changing relationships.
    ISBN 0-7398-6424-6 (lib. bdg.)
    1. Puberty--Juvenile literature. [1. Puberty.]
  I. Title. II. Series.
  QP84.4.E43 2004
  612.6'61--dc21

                              2003003711

Acknowledgments
The author and publishers thank the following for their permission to reproduce photographs and illustrations: Cover, pp.1, 28, 30, 31, 33, 35, 37, 39, 45, 47, 49, 56, 59 Corbis Images: cover, pp. 1 45 (Nancy Ney), p.28 (Will and Deni McIntyre), p.30 (Tom Stewart Photography), p.31 (David R. Stoecklein Photography), p.33 (Paul Barton), p.35 (Roy Morsch), p.37 (Ed Bock Photography, Inc.), p.39 (Mug Shots), p.47 (Tom Stewart Photography), p.49 (Tom Stewart Photography), p.56 (Julian Hirshowitz), p.59 (Jon Feingersh); pp.3, 8(top), 40, 57 Photofusion: pp. 3, 8t, 40 (Paul Baldesare), 57 (Christa Stadtler); pp.4, 5, 8b, 13, 21, 26, 42, 53, 55 Angela Hampton Family Life Picture Library; p.7(bottom) Impact Photos (Nigel Barklie); pp.6, 15 Science Photo Library: p.6 (Sidney Moulds), p.15 (Professors P. M. Motta and J. Van Blerkom); pp.7(top), 17, 50, 54 Topham/ImageWorks; p.19(top) Topham/UPPA.co.uk; pp.22 (top and bottom), 24 Hodder Wayland Picture Library; p.51 Topham/Chapman.
The illustrations by Michael Courtney on pages 14, 19b and 20, and the are from the Hodder Wayland Picture Library.
The illustration on page 27 is by Carole Binding.
Note: Photographs illustrating the case studies in this book were posed by models.

Contents

Introduction
What Is Puberty?

Puberty is the name given to some important physical changes that occur during adolescence. In humans this is somewhere between the ages of 8 and 18. Although you have been growing and changing ever since you were born, the changes that happen around this time are more dramatic and mark the time when you stop being a child and start to become an adult.

The most significant change is that your body becomes capable of reproduction—that is, able to produce babies. Chapter 1 explains what all the changes are, when and how they happen, and how they might affect your day-to-day life.

It's important to stay healthy during this time, because your body has a lot of extra work to do and needs a good supply of nutrients and energy. Paying attention to diet, exercise, rest, and personal care will make you feel healthy. Chapter 2 provides information and advice to help you with this.

Once you start to become sexually mature, you may find that you spend more and more time thinking about sex and relationships. In particular, you may develop a crush on someone, and you may fall in love for the first time. This can be scary, especially when you are not really sure what is going on and how you are supposed to behave. Chapter 3 looks at how the physical changes that occur at puberty can affect your relationships. Chapter 3 also looks at the dangers that may be faced by a young person who is physically more mature than he or she is emotionally.

About to change
In about five years, these three children turned into the young adults on page 5. Leaving childhood behind can be a scary experience.

As well as the physical changes, you will start to feel different emotionally. This is because your body is undergoing a major upheaval. Your priorities, friendships, and interests are changing. You might suddenly feel shy in the company of other people, embarrassed about things that are happening to you, or worried that you are not "normal." Sometimes, it seems as if you don't even know yourself any more. This can be unsettling, making you feel miserable, confused, and even angry. All this is, in fact, perfectly normal, and although it may not seem so at the moment, the difficulties will pass quickly and you will be ready to cope with being a young adult. Chapter 4 looks at this in more detail.

Adolescence can be an anxious and uncertain time, but it can also be very exciting. This book is meant to help reassure you that what is happening to you during puberty is normal, to give you information on what is likely to happen next, and to help you understand your feelings about becoming an adult.

Ready for the future

Understanding the changes that happen during puberty helps teenagers to develop into happy, confident young adults.

1 Physical Changes
The Power of Hormones

How puberty begins

Puberty begins as a result of the action of hormones, which circulate in your bloodstream like messengers telling different parts of the body what to do. The average age for starting puberty is 11 for girls and 13 for boys, but anywhere between 8 and 17 for girls and 10 and 18 for boys is within the normal range. The age at which puberty begins for you depends largely on the characteristics you inherited from your parents. Every cell in the human body contains 46 chromosomes (23 from each parent). These tiny thread-like structures carry the "code" or "recipe" for how our bodies develop. This means that we are biologically programmed to start puberty at a certain time—usually a similar time to that of one or both of our parents. When that time is reached, the hormones start to do their work.

An area of the brain called the hypothalamus produces gonadotropin-releasing hormone (GnRH). This stimulates the pituitary gland to release follicle-stimulating hormone (FSH) and luteinizing hormone (LH). These hormones prompt the gonads (testes in boys and ovaries in girls) to produce the sex hormones.

In boys high levels of the hormone testosterone are secreted. In girls the ovaries start to produce high levels of estrogen and progesterone. These sex hormones help the testes and ovaries to continue maturing and bring about the other changes of puberty. They trigger the production of sperm in boys and the release of ova (eggs) in girls. This is what makes reproduction possible.

Testosterone
A micrograph of a crystal of testosterone. Levels of this hormone increase at puberty in both boys and girls, but the increase is particularly large in boys.

Girls: a quick guide to what happens when

Remember that these are approximate ages only.

10–11 Breasts start to "bud," one sometimes starts to grow before the other; growth spurt begins.

11–12 Pubic hair grows along the lips of the vagina, gradually spreading up and out, becoming coarser, darker, and curlier.

12–13 Body fat increases, especially around the hips; breasts continue to grow; underarm hair appears and sweating becomes more obvious, taking on a different odor. Some girls develop acne. There may be a discharge of mucus from the vagina shortly before menstruation (periods) begins.

14–15 In most girls, breasts are almost fully developed by the age of 15. Periods have usually started though may not be regular at first. Breasts may be sore just before a period, and abdominal cramps may occur.

15–16 Physical growth is usually completed, although emotional changes can continue until 19 or 20.

The way you look
Don't worry, you will soon get used to your changing look and shape.

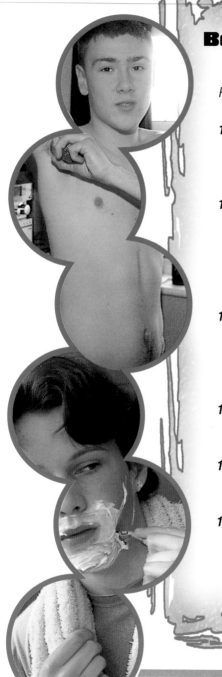

Boys: a quick guide to what happens when

Remember that these are approximate ages only.

11–12 Testicles begin to grow. The right is often larger than the left, which sits slightly lower in the scrotum. Growth spurt begins.

12–13 Penis starts to grow. Pubic hair appears around the base of the penis. Underarm hair appears and odor develops. There may be a slight enlargement of the breast tissue under one or both nipples. This is normal and will disappear eventually.

13–14 Pubic hair spreads up and out, and the penis continues to grow. The chest and shoulders become broader. Some boys experience nocturnal emissions (wet dreams) around this time.

14–15 Voice begins to deepen. Some boys develop acne. There may be first signs of facial hair.

15–16 The penis and testicles are almost fully developed. Chest and shoulders are more muscular.

16–17 Physical growth is completed in some boys, but many continue to grow for another year or two. They may get taller or more broad-chested and muscular. Emotional changes may continue for a further two or three years.

Personal care

A more "adult" smell and facial hair growth may mean that it takes much longer to prepare for an evening out.

Delayed puberty

Occasionally, someone passes the normal age range for starting puberty without showing any signs of it, or they start puberty and then it stops progressing. This is known as delayed puberty. There are several causes of delayed puberty:

 Some illnesses (e.g., cystic fibrosis and kidney disease) can make it harder for the body to grow and develop.

 Eating disorders such as anorexia nervosa can result in the body being undernourished, and this inhibits growth and development.

 Rarely, excessive exercise, such as in the case of professional athletes, gymnasts, and ballet dancers, can delay puberty in girls. It can prevent the body from gaining the amount of body fat required for menstruation to begin.

 Abnormalities in the chromosomes or problems with the production of hormones.

Many people who think they have delayed puberty are just "late bloomers." However, if you are concerned, you should see a doctor. The doctor may ask about your family's growth patterns and your medical history, and may do some blood tests. If a physical problem is suspected, you may be referred to an endocrinologist (a specialist in growth problems). It is possible that hormones will be prescribed. This would consist of testosterone for boys and pills containing estrogen for girls. Girls may also need to take growth hormones. Usually puberty starts without help, but when a teenager is very upset by the situation, hormone treatment may be suggested. Correct management of any illness you may have, as well as a balanced diet, will help make sure that your body has the resources to grow and develop properly.

Left behind?

Being the only one in your class who hasn't started puberty can be difficult, especially if the other kids tease or laugh at you. If you're having problems at school, or feel unhappy or depressed, talk to your parents, teacher, or doctor. Even if you know you'll catch up soon, you may need a little extra support while you're waiting.

Precocious puberty

With precocious puberty someone undergoes the physical changes of puberty before the usual age range. The main problem with starting puberty early is that, if it also finishes early, the skeleton will mature too quickly. Bones stop growing when puberty ends. This means that, while children with precocious puberty may seem tall for their age, their bones stop growing sooner and they may not reach their full height potential. This is only a problem when the "bone age" is abnormally advanced. Often, while there may be outward signs of early puberty such as early breast development or early appearance of pubic hair, the bone age will be normal.

"I started puberty in grade school. I looked older than my classmates, but in my head I felt the same as them. I was only 8. It was embarrassing and people's remarks were sometimes mean."
(Roxanne, age 13)

Treatment is not necessary in the majority of cases, but bone growth should be monitored. This is usually done by X-ray. If the doctor finds that bone age is unusually advanced, a hormone treatment to halt the process may be recommended. Daily or monthly injections of a drug containing synthetic growth hormones are given until the age of 11–12 in girls and 12–13 in boys, when puberty is allowed to continue.

In most cases, there is no obvious reason for early puberty, although it may run in families. It's more common in girls and in overweight children. Other possible but rarer causes include problems with the pituitary or thyroid glands, or tumors in the brain, testes, or ovaries.

Growth spurt

One of the earliest physical changes to occur at puberty is the growth spurt, which starts around the age of 10–11 in girls, 12–13 in boys. Growth is triggered in both boys and girls by an increase in levels of the hormone testosterone.

At each end of the long bones (those longer than they are wide, for example, the arms, legs, hands, and feet) there is a soft area of bone that is separated from the main shaft by a plate of a rubbery substance called cartilage. Cartilage grows throughout childhood, gradually lengthening the bones. The process speeds up at puberty, under the influence of hormones. At the end of puberty, the cartilage ossifies (hardens into bone) and you stop growing. One reason why women tend to be smaller than men is that they usually mature earlier, which means that their bones stop growing sooner.

The period of rapid growth starts with the hands and feet. Then your arms and legs get longer and finally the spine grows and you will realize how much taller you are. You may grow 2–5 in (6–12 cm) in height in a year. One problem with such a height increase is that your brain finds it hard to keep up with the speed of your growth. You may suddenly find that you cannot balance properly and keep falling over. Clumsiness is common in people who are growing quickly.

Growth rates

Teenagers develop at very different rates. You may be much shorter or taller than your classmates.

In most cases, the age at which you start your growth spurt makes no difference to your eventual height. Most girls finish growing by the age of 17, while boys may continue to grow until 19 or 20. The rate of growth varies from person to person, so you might be considerably taller or shorter than others your age.

As well as getting taller, your body shape changes. Girls begin to develop breasts, broader hips, and generally a more rounded, curvy shape. Boys begin to develop broader shoulders and a more muscular chest.

Body hair and genitals

Soon after your shape begins to change, you will start to grow pubic hair. This tends to be soft and straight at first, and appears in a line down the center of the pubic area. This is the area covering the pubic bone, which is found at the front of the pelvis, just behind the genitals. In girls, the pubic hair spreads out to form an inverted triangle, possibly extending slightly down the inside of the legs. For boys, the pubic hair spreads out to form a diamond shape, and may cover the testicles. It may extend slightly down the inside of the legs. For both sexes the hair becomes coarser and curlier, and might be a different shade from the hair on the head.

"When I started to get hair around my penis, it was straight and in little tufts. I knew it was supposed to be curly, but I didn't realize that would happen later." (Mark, age 14)

Underarm hair tends to appear a year or two later, as does hair on other parts of the body, such as arms, legs, abdomen, and chest. Girls often grow a few hairs around the nipples. Boys will begin to grow hair on the chin and upper lip, although this may not happen until two or three years after puberty begins.

You will also notice changes in the size and shape of your genitals. In boys, the testicles become larger and a year or so later the penis increases in size. In girls, the lips of the vagina (labia) become larger. It is not unusual for one lip to be larger than the other, or for the inner lips to protrude.

What else happens to girls?

The development of the breasts is one of the earliest changes of puberty, and along with the onset of monthly periods, one of the most important. A woman's breasts are developed to produce milk for any babies she may have.

The growth of breast tissue is stimulated by the hormone estrogen, which is produced by the ovaries. The first thing you notice, usually at around age 10 or 11, is that your nipples begin to bud or get bigger. The surrounding area gradually enlarges and develops. Sometimes, one breast develops faster than the other, and this is nothing to worry about. Breasts usually end up roughly the same size, although no woman's breasts are identical.

It's important to buy a bra that will give plenty of support and comfort, especially when you are playing sports. There are many different types available, including strong sports bras. Even if your breasts have not started to develop, you may decide you would like to wear a small bra or a "training bra."

The perfect fit!

Many stores have trained fitters who can measure you for a bra, and this is the ideal way to get a perfect fit.

My breasts are too big

Claire is 14, and her breasts are already well developed. "They started to grow when I was ten," she says. "I was the only one in my class who started to develop and I hated it. I still do. It feels like everyone's staring at my chest all the time, especially when I walk, because they bounce all over the place. I always try to get out of playing sports because I know that if I jump around, my breasts will hurt and my classmates will laugh at me." A sports bra might be a good solution for Claire.

It's common to worry about the size of your breasts, but for every girl who wishes her breasts were bigger, there's another who wishes hers were smaller. You may also worry that they are too round or too pointy, or that your nipples are too flat or too prominent. Breasts come in all shapes and sizes, just like the rest of our bodies, and you should not be misled by magazine pictures of "ideal" figures (see Chapter 2).

Periods (menstruation)

For girls, the onset of periods, usually about 18 months after the development of breasts, is the major change that occurs at puberty. It means that they are now capable of becoming pregnant. Periods are part of a process called the menstrual cycle, by which the uterus (or womb) prepares itself for the implantation of a fertilized ovum (egg), the first stage in the development of a baby. The complete menstrual cycle takes about four weeks.

Myth | Fact

Exercise will make your breasts bigger.

Breasts do not contain any muscle, so exercise cannot affect their size. The chest muscles, which support the breasts, can be strengthened through exercise, and this may prevent the breasts from drooping in later life.

fallopian tube

uterus

ovary

cervix

vagina

A monthly process

Each month an egg is released from one of the ovaries and travels along the fallopian tube. If fertilized by a sperm, it attaches itself to the lining of the uterus, which has thickened in preparation for this.

What happens during the menstrual cycle?

A period is the name given to the expulsion through the vagina of the lining of the uterus. This occurs every four weeks, if an ovum has not been fertilized by a sperm. At the same time, FSH (follicle-stimulating hormone) from the pituitary gland causes a new ovum to start to mature inside a follicle in the ovary.

By about day five, the period will be over and the follicle containing the maturing ovum moves to the surface of the ovary. The follicle produces the hormone estrogen, which causes the lining of the uterus to start to thicken.

Halfway through the cycle (day 14), the pituitary gland starts to produce LH (luteinizing hormone) instead of FSH. This causes the now-mature ovum to burst out of its follicle and travel through the fallopian tube and into the uterus. This is called ovulation. Progesterone produced by the follicle makes the thickening lining of the uterus soft and spongy, ready to receive the ovum if it is fertilized.

Normal cycles

When you start to have periods, they may not happen regularly. Once things have settled down, you'll probably have a period lasting between three and seven days every 28 days or so. This can vary, though; a normal cycle may be anything between 21 and 35 days. The description on this page is only an average.

Ovulation

This colored electron micrograph shows an ovum (pink) that has burst out of its follicle and is rolling down the surface of the ovary.

By day 21, if the ovum has not been fertilized, it begins to disintegrate along with the thickened lining of the uterus, which starts to come away from the uterine walls, causing some of the tiny blood vessels to tear as it does so. Estrogen and progesterone levels fall, and the mixture of uterine cells, blood, and mucus is released through the vagina as a period. The whole cycle then begins again.

Discharge

A clear or milky discharge from the vagina is normal both during and after puberty. Some girls experience a whitish discharge for a few months before their periods start, which is a useful "early-warning" sign. If your normal discharge becomes thick and smells unpleasant, especially if you have any itching or burning when you urinate, you may have an infection. Yeast infections are very common and have many causes, including perfumed soaps, antibiotics, or just being tired. If you're sexually active, it's possible that you may have a sexually transmitted disease (STD). Whatever the cause, you should seek medical advice.

Managing your periods

Many girls worry that they'll start their periods suddenly while they're away from home. In fact, you'll probably notice a little blood when you go to the bathroom, and this will give you time to find some sanitary protection. You could carry a sanitary pad with you, to be ready. Many public toilets have coin-operated dispensers.

You may feel anxious and self-conscious at first, and some girls worry that others will know that they have their period. Sanitary protection is not noticeable, and there's no need for anyone to know. However, you may find that talking about your periods and sharing your concerns with friends is helpful and reassuring for all of you.

Pads or tampons?

Sanitary pads (also known as pads, napkins, or maxi-pads) are absorbent pads worn inside your underwear to soak up the menstrual flow as it leaves the body. They have an adhesive strip along the back to keep them in place, and may have "wings"—sticky flaps that tuck around your underwear for extra security. Tampons are inserted into the vagina and absorb the menstrual flow from inside. Both pads and tampons come in a range of thicknesses and absorbencies to allow for variation in the flow of the period.

Menstrual blood has no smell until it comes into contact with the air, where it combines with bacteria and may cause an odor. You should change your pad every few hours to stay feeling fresh and comfortable.

Many girls prefer to use pads at first, although you can use tampons with your first period. A tampon cannot get lost inside you, but you must remember to take each one out before inserting another. It is also important to change tampons at least every four to six hours as they can cause infection if left in for too long. An infection called toxic shock syndrome, though rare, can be very serious.

Myth

If a tampon tears your hymen (the tough membrane partially covering the entrance to the vagina), you are no longer a virgin.

Fact

A virgin is someone who has never had sexual intercourse. The hymen is usually broken during first sex, but it is possible that using a tampon could break it. The hymen is tougher in some girls than in others and some are born without one. Whether your hymen is broken or not, you are a virgin until you have sexual intercourse.

Using a tampon

"I wanted to use tampons but I couldn't get them in, so I gave up and used pads. A year later I tried tampons again. I managed to insert one this time, but I could still feel it, so I knew it wasn't in right. In the end, my big sister gave me some great tips. She said you should start with the smallest size when your period is at its heaviest. They're easier to insert that way. Then, once you've had some practice, you can try at the start of your period. You have to relax, too. Once you've done it a few times, it's easier."
(Mia, age 15)

Problem periods

It's not unusual to experience irregularities in the first few years of menstruation when hormone levels are unsettled. If a period problem is worrying you, or preventing you from getting on with life as normal, your doctor can help.

Problem	Causes	What can be done
Painful periods (dysmenorrhea) cramp like pains or a dull ache in the lower abdomen, usually in the first day or two of the period.	*Possibly a result of hormones causing the uterus to contract. Occasionally due to growths in the uterus or to pelvic inflammation.*	*Gentle exercise, painkillers, and lying with a hot-water bottle on your stomach may help. Your doctor may prescribe a hormone pill to treat your period pains.*
Heavy periods (menorrhagia) lasting longer than seven days or requiring more than one pad an hour. This can lead to anemia (see page 35).	*Often due to a hormone imbalance that causes the lining of the uterus to keep building up, resulting in a heavier period. Occasionally, heavy bleeding is due to growths, inflammation, or infection.*	*Your doctor may suggest hormone treatment. Infections or growths may require medication or surgery.*
Irregular periods common in the first year or so. Some months you may not have a period.	*Fluctuating hormone levels may be responsible. If you're sexually active and miss a period, you may be pregnant.*	*Not knowing when you're "due" can be a problem, so carry a pad or tampon with you. Usually periods regulate themselves eventually, but in some cases hormone treatment may be recommended.*
Absence of periods (amenorrhea) when you haven't started by age 16 (primary) or when your periods stop after a few months (secondary).	*Hormones are probably to blame, although pregnancy is possible in girls who are sexually active. Hormone levels can be affected by stress, weight loss, excessive exercise, thyroid problems, or ovarian cysts.*	*Hormone therapy may get things going again. A balanced diet and avoiding excessive exercise may also help.*
PMS (pre menstrual stress) feeling irritable, tired, depressed, and tearful in the days before your period; also bloating and sore breasts.	*Probably due to a sudden fall in progesterone and estrogen levels a week or so before your period. These hormones affect the levels of endorphins ("feel-good" chemicals) in the brain.*	*Symptoms usually disappear once the period starts. In the meantime, concentrate on eating a balanced diet and getting regular, gentle exercise. Some nutritional supplements may be effective.*

What else happens to boys?

Voice changes

The male sex hormone testosterone, which is responsible for the physical changes we have already looked at, also affects the voice. It triggers the growth of the larynx (voice box) and the lengthening of the vocal cords. The larger the larynx, the deeper the voice. As the larynx gets bigger, it begins to stick out, and we call the bump it makes the "Adam's apple." As with every other part of the body, the size of the Adam's apple varies from person to person. As you get older and your body fills out, the bump is likely to become much less prominent.

Some boys are worried about their voice "breaking" or getting deeper. They find it embarrassing when they start talking in the voice they know as their own, then suddenly find that it's going from squeaky to deep in the same sentence. This happens because the muscles in the larynx may weaken or "wobble" during this period of growth. Try not to be embarrassed. This happens to most boys, and at some time, it happened to most men, including your dad, your favorite ball player, actor, pop star, or politician. It doesn't last for long, and very soon your voice will stay the same all the time.

New notes
A choirboy's high, clear tone will disappear as his voice breaks. Many choirboys continue to sing, but as part of an adult choir.

Larynx
The larynx or voice box is situated in the middle of the front of the neck. You can feel it move up and down when you swallow.

larynx

Involuntary erections and wet dreams

The proper name for wet dreams is "nocturnal emissions." "Nocturnal" means night, and "emission" means to send out or discharge, so this simply means the discharge of fluid (called semen) from the penis which sometimes happens while you are asleep at night—although it would be the same thing if it occurred during a daytime nap.

Wet dreams happen during puberty when the production of sperm in the testes is at its highest, because of the increased levels of testosterone. In some boys, this causes more frequent erections (when the penis becomes bigger and stiffer and stands upright) and ejaculation, which is another word for emission of semen from the penis. Sometimes, this happens in response to a dream. At other times, you may

"At first I thought I'd wet the bed, then I realized what it was. I was so embarrassed, though. What if my mom saw it on the sheets? I just wiped it with a wet cloth and now I wear underwear to bed, just in case!"
(Jay, age 15)

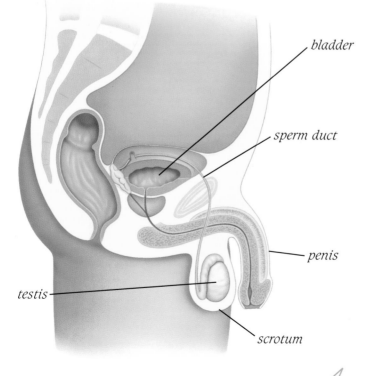

bladder

sperm duct

penis

testis

scrotum

Where sperm are produced

Sperm are produced in the testis and then travel, in semen, through the sperm duct.

find you've had a wet dream although you don't remember dreaming anything at all. It can be frightening to wake up and find the bed wet. Some boys assume they have wet themselves or that they are bleeding. A quick check confirms that it's not blood or urine. Semen is usually whitish, and may be thin and watery or fairly thick. Some boys worry about having wet dreams, and many more worry that they haven't had one. The thing to remember is that whether you do or whether you don't, you are perfectly normal.

Involuntary erections are one of the most common embarassments of puberty. It is common to have an erection while you're in the shower, or when you see other boys naked in the locker room. Sometimes, just seeing naked bodies is enough to cause an erection. If you get an erection when Great Aunt Mary visits, your mind may be wandering without your realizing it. Try to just think about something boring, and your erection will eventually go away.

Embarrassing erections

Matt is 14, and he's getting fed up with his body's behavior. "My penis seems to have a mind of its own! I can't stop getting erections—it's so embarrassing. Last week I was taking a shower with the other guys after gym class, and I got this huge hard-on. I just had to stand facing the wall until it went down."

2 Looking After Yourself

How to Stay Fit and Look Good

Most children tend to take their bodies for granted. They eat the foods their parents provide, they take a bath when they are told to, and, if they feel ill, someone will call the doctor or put them to bed and take care of them. During puberty, your body faces a number of challenges, from pimples or mood swings, due to hormonal activity, to the threat of damage from injury as you try new things. It may not seem fair that, just when you have to start taking more responsibility for looking after your own body, it seems to get harder to look after.

Keeping clean

During puberty, your skin starts to produce more sebum, the oily substance that protects it and keeps it supple (see more about this on page 24). You will also start to sweat more, even when you don't

A new regime
In the past your parents may have had to drag you into the bathroom. Now they may have to drag you out of it!

feel hot. Sweating is one of the ways in which your body gets rids of waste. In addition, your skin is constantly renewing itself, with the top layer (the epidermis) shedding dead cells as new cells form. A buildup of dead skin, sebum, and sweat can smell unpleasant, so you will need to take a bath or shower more often than when you were younger.

You will sweat more in hot weather and when you are nervous or excited, especially under the arms and around the genitals where there are more sweat glands. After washing your armpits, you may want to use a deodorant or antiperspirant to keep you feeling fresh.

Washing "down below"

It's important to wash the genital area at least once a day to prevent bacteria from entering the body through the penis, vagina, or urethra (the tube that carries urine from the bladder). This is one of the causes of bladder infections, although there are many others. Girls should always wipe and wash from front to back to avoid getting bacteria from the rectum in contact with the vaginal area.

Circumcision

Circumcision is an operation in which the foreskin—the skin that covers the glans or head of the penis—is removed. In the United States, many baby boys are circumcised at birth in the hospital. Some religions, such as Judaism and Islam, require boys to be circumcised in a special ceremony.

In boys and men who are not circumcised, a white, creamy substance called smegma, which helps the skin to slide back easily over the glans, can build up under the foreskin and can become smelly. If you are not circumcised, make sure that you clean under your foreskin regularly to avoid this happening.

Some boys find that when their body develops at puberty their foreskin is too tight. This also makes erections uncomfortable. If your foreskin feels tight, you should discuss this with your doctor.

Coping with acne

There are different types of acne but by far the most common is *acne vulgaris*, which is the type usually seen in adolescents. It is caused by the overproduction of sebum by the skin's sebaceous glands. Sebum keeps your skin supple and waterproof. Overproduction of sebum is triggered by the raised levels of testosterone at puberty. Excess sebum, dead skin cells, and bacteria build up on the skin, blocking the pores. The bacteria then cause an infection and pimples form as a result. Girls produce less testosterone than boys, making boys more prone to acne. There are more sebaceous glands on the face and back, which is why acne is worse in these areas.

Myth | **Fact**

Eating chocolate gives you pimples. | *No food can give you pimples (unless you have an allergy). A balanced, healthy diet will help give you a glowing, fresh complexion.*

In most cases, acne is unpleasant but tolerable, and can be kept under control until it disappears naturally. In some cases, however, it can be severe and painful and can leave scars. If your acne is seriously affecting your life, see your doctor. It can usually be treated, although this can take several months.

Toby gets help

Toby is 15. He started to get a few pimples about six months ago and, though he cleaned the area twice a day, they kept getting worse. "In the end, I didn't even want to go to school," says Toby. "The other kids called me 'pizza face.' As one pimple went, another would appear. They hurt, too. In the end, my dad made me go to the doctor. She prescribed some cream and pills, and it started to improve within a couple of weeks."

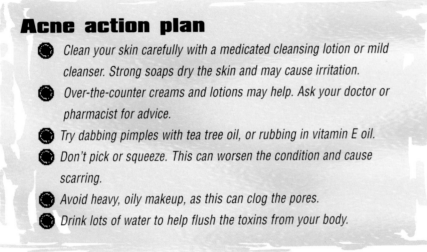

Acne action plan

- Clean your skin carefully with a medicated cleansing lotion or mild cleanser. Strong soaps dry the skin and may cause irritation.
- Over-the-counter creams and lotions may help. Ask your doctor or pharmacist for advice.
- Try dabbing pimples with tea tree oil, or rubbing in vitamin E oil.
- Don't pick or squeeze. This can worsen the condition and cause scarring.
- Avoid heavy, oily makeup, as this can clog the pores.
- Drink lots of water to help flush the toxins from your body.

Boys and facial hair

When hair starts to appear on the face toward the end of puberty, it may be quite soft—more of a "facial fluff." It usually starts on the upper lip, then spreads to the cheeks and finally the chin. Some boys find this small amount of facial hair embarrassing, and may prefer to start shaving before there is much growth.

Girls and excess hair

It's normal for girls to grow hair on their legs, abdomen, chin, upper lip, and around the nipples, in addition to pubic and underarm hair. Some girls prefer to remove or lighten body hair; others are happy to leave it. Many women remove hair from their legs regularly, by shaving, using creams, or waxing. Odd stray hairs on the chin or around the nipples can be carefully plucked out with tweezers.

"I'm quite a hairy person. I don't mind having hairy arms, but I shave my legs, especially if I go swimming." (Cara, age 14)

Most people have hair on their upper lip. If it's fine and light in color, you probably won't even notice it. In some girls, however, it's dark and quite thick. If this bothers you, you could use a facial hair-removal cream, or you could try products that lighten the hair, making it less

How to shave

It's probably quickest and easiest to use an electric razor, but some people prefer an ordinary razor with shaving cream and warm water. They say this gives a closer shave. To use an ordinary razor, you should wet your skin slightly and then apply shaving cream to the area to be shaved; girls should do one leg at a time. Shave against the direction of the hair growth, rinsing the razor frequently. Make sure your razor blade is sharp and don't try to shave too quickly, or you may cut yourself. After shaving, boys may want to use after-shave lotion, to close the pores on the face. For girls, a little moisturizer keeps legs soft. Shaving off the ends of the hairs makes them blunt and this is why they may appear coarse or stubbly when they grow again.

noticeable. You should talk to your parents or a skin care specialist about the best way to deal with unwanted hair. Many of the products available contain harsh chemicals, so you should get help from an adult in choosing a safe one. Girls should not shave facial hair, as this will make the hair seem coarser and more noticeable.

Occasionally, excess hair growth (hirsutism) is due to a hormonal imbalance. There are some medical conditions associated with this, for example, polycystic ovary syndrome (PCOS) where multiple cysts form on the ovaries. If you are worried about excess hair, talk to your doctor.

Smile please!
Uneven teeth can usually be straightened by wearing braces.

Teeth

Bacteria can build up on the teeth, causing tooth decay and gum disease. To avoid this, clean your teeth when you get up and before you go to bed. Ask your dentist how to do this properly. From the age of about six or seven, your "milk" or baby teeth will have been gradually replaced by permanent or "adult" teeth. By the age of 12 or 13, you will have most of your adult teeth. If they have come in a little crooked, you could see an orthodontist, who specializes in straightening the teeth. You may be advised to wear braces, which put pressure on your teeth to help them move into the right position. It usually takes a year or two to achieve the perfect smile, but braces now are much less noticeable than they used to be. They are made with smaller wires and are more comfortable, and you can even get them in different colors.

Eating healthily

It's important to eat a balanced diet at any age, but it's especially important during puberty since your body is coping with major changes, including the growth spurt. A balanced diet means one that includes a variety of foods from the different food groups. Although not everyone agrees with it, the U.S. government's "food pyramid" is a quick way of showing how much you should eat from each group: more from the largest group at the bottom and less from the smallest group at the top.

Starchy carbohydrates are a source of energy. They should make up the bulk of your diet. However, it is important that you eat whole grains, such as whole wheat bread, and not fill up on processed foods such as sugared cereals and white bread.

Food pyramid
This is the food pyramid recommended by the U.S. government. Some nutritionists have other ideas about how to best structure your eating.

Vegetables and fruits provide your body with vitamins and minerals, plus fiber, which helps keep your bowels regular and protects against colon cancer. Fruit and vegetables

Fit food!

There's an old saying that "you are what you eat." Fresh healthy foods can make you feel full of energy and glowing with fitness, while too many chips or doughnuts will make you sluggish and lethargic.

also give you energy and boost the immune system, the body's natural illness-protection. Some vegetables, especially greens and broccoli, are good sources of calcium and iron. Iron is particularly important for girls, as menstruation increases the body's iron requirements. You should eat at least five servings of fruit and vegetables each day. A serving may not be as much as you think. An example of one serving is one medium apple or banana, one large carrot, or a medium portion of salad or greens.

Dairy products (milk, cheese and yogurt) provide calcium for strong, healthy bones and teeth. They also provide protein for growth. The biggest sources of protein are meat and poultry, fish, eggs, nuts, and legumes such as lentils and beans. Both protein and calcium are especially important in puberty when your body is growing rapidly. You should eat two servings from each of these groups a day. One container of low-fat yogurt, two ounces of cheese, one egg, four ounces of cooked lean meat or fish, or a small portion of lentils would all be considered one serving.

At the top of the pyramid is the group from which you should eat sparingly. Sweets, cakes, and cookies have little nutritional value. Although sugar can give you instant energy, levels fall again quickly, and you feel more tired so keep sugar intake low.

There are two main types of fat. Saturated fats are found in animal products such as meat, butter, margarine, lard, and cream. Eating too much of this kind of fat can lead to heart disease and weight problems. Unsaturated fats are found in some margarines, vegetable oils, and nuts. Studies suggest that olive oil may protect against illnesses such as heart disease and colon cancer. Your body needs some fat, so avoid saturated fats where possible and eat unsaturated fats in moderation.

Calories

A calorie is a unit of energy. Different foods have different numbers of calories and provide different amounts of energy. When you are going through puberty, your body needs extra calories to cope. Generally, males need more calories than females, as their bodies tend to be bigger and use more energy.

Shape and size and weight

At puberty, your body gradually lays down more fat. Girls in particular will notice extra fat around the hips and stomach. This is because females are designed to have babies and the fat stores can be drawn upon during pregnancy. Girls are naturally rounder than boys, but some girls think this means they are fat—especially if they judge themselves by unrealistic images they see in magazines. Boys may worry that they're not as tall, as slim, as broad-chested, or as muscular as the men they see in magazines.

Fact

It is estimated that in the United States 1 in 25 women between the ages of 15 and 35 have an eating disorder. Approximately 10 percent of people with eating disorders are men.

If your size and shape don't match up to magazine pictures, remember this. Every model who appears in print is chosen from a large selection of models. The photographer spends several hours taking hundreds of pictures. Magazine editors and designers choose the best picture, which is then fed into a computer. The design team then manipulates the image until it's perfect. This may include enhancing eye size and color and getting rid of blemishes. In women, the shape and size of the model's waist, bottom, legs, and bust is usually altered, and in men, the width of the chest may be increased, the skin may be made darker, and the size and shape of muscles on the arms, legs, chest, and abdomen may be enhanced.

If you weigh considerably more than a friend of similar age and height, you may need to talk to your doctor about losing weight or allowing your body to "grow into" its weight. Following healthy eating recommendations should prevent you from becoming too fat or too thin. Continuing healthy eating habits as you grow older can protect you against many cancers as well as heart disease and bone problems.

A true picture?
Computer software has enabled a designer to alter the shape, skin tones, and other details of the people in this photo. Notice how in the picture on the right the woman's bust and the man's chest are both larger than they are in the original version of the picture.

If your body uses fewer calories than you eat, the surplus is stored as fat, so you should only eat as many calories as your body needs—fewer if you're overweight. The best way to do this is to cut down on foods that are very high in calories, such as sweets and fried food, and fill up on nutritious food that is lower in calories. If you increase the amount of exercise you do, your body will use more calories so fewer calories will be stored as fat.

Exercise

Lack of exercise is an increasing problem in the United States, particularly among children and young people. There are a number of reasons for this. Often parents who are worried about their children's

The benefits of exercise

- builds up your muscles
- strengthens your heart
- improves your circulation
- increases your stamina
- keeps your joints supple
- improves your breathing
- helps keep your weight under control
- prevents you from feeling depressed

No longer a couch potato!
Bicycling, running, swimming, tennis, gymnastics, and dance are all forms of aerobic exercise that can be done gently or vigorously.

safety insist on driving them to and from school. Driving rather than walking then becomes a habit that is hard to break later on. More television channels, good-quality video and DVD recordings, computer games, and the Internet mean that the number of teenagers playing sports outside of school has fallen as kids opt for less-active leisure pursuits. Health experts talk about the rise in teenage "couch potatoes." Insufficient exercise can have long-term consequences, including obesity, heart disease, and problems with bones and joints.

"I like TV and computer games, but I do other stuff as well. If you sit around all the time, you'll get fat and then you get out of breath if you try to run or anything."
(Marcus, age 12)

So how do you stay fit and healthy? You should aim to do some form of aerobic exercise for 20–30 minutes, three or four times a week. Aerobic exercise is low-intensity, long-duration exercise where you maintain 60–80 percent of your maximum heartrate for at least 15 minutes. Swimming, walking, bicycling, and jogging are some examples. During aerobic exercise, you should be able to hold a conversation. If you're gasping for breath, you are probably doing anaerobic exercise, which is high-intensity and short-duration, such as sprinting or weightlifting.

Some people in highly competitive sports exercise to excess. Too much exercise can result in low body weight, which can affect development and may delay puberty (see Chapter 1).

Exercise and your heart rate

A normal heart rate is about 70 beats per minute. During exercise, your body needs extra oxygen, so your heartrate speeds up in order to pump blood (which carries oxygen) around the body more quickly. A person's maximum heartrate is calculated by subtracting his or her age from the number 220. So at age 15, your maximum heartrate is 205 beats per minute. It would be dangerous for your heart to speed up more than this. In aerobic exercise the heartrate stays at 60–80 percent of the maximum. So, at age 15, this would be 123–164 beats per minute.

Teenage health problems

An existing health problem, or one that develops around puberty, can seem difficult as you become more independent. You are probably taking responsibility for things that your parents looked after before. For example, you now need to keep track of your own medical treatment, such as using an inhaler or injecting insulin, and you need to be able to recognize and avoid situations or activities that could make your condition worse. It may be embarrassing if, occasionally, your condition means that you shouldn't join in with an activity. If you explain, you'll probably find that friends are interested and will help accomodate your needs. It is also a good idea to make sure that friends know what to do in an emergency.

Leisure time
Having a long-term health problem doesn't have to keep you from having fun.

Accepting diabetes

"I think my mom worries more about my diabetes than I do. She's always worrying about what I eat and whether I've got my medication with me. She's calming down now, though. I think she realizes she has to trust me to look after myself. My friends used to think it was really gross that I had to inject myself, but now they totally accept it. You get funny looks if you do it in public—people think you are shooting up heroin or something, but that's their problem. Having diabetes can be a pain sometimes, but that's the way it is and you just get used to it."
(Kyla, age 15)

Diabetes

There are two types of diabetes. In Type 1, the body stops producing a hormone called insulin, which is essential for controlling the level of sugar in the blood. People with Type 1 diabetes rely on insulin injections to survive. In Type 2 diabetes, the body produces insulin but either the amount may not be enough or the body does not react properly to it.

Most young people who have diabetes have Type 1. As well as injecting themselves with insulin, they need to monitor their blood sugar level by doing regular blood tests. To keep their blood sugar level as constant as possible, people with both types of diabetes need to eat regularly and be careful about what they eat. They also need to be careful to increase the amount they eat if they are taking extra exercise and using extra energy.

If you are diabetic, you will probably find that your insulin needs change during puberty, since the body's ability to use insulin is reduced by the effect of growth hormones. Also, some girls find that menstruation affects their blood sugar levels.

Epilepsy

People with epilepsy frequently have seizures. A seizure happens when messages don't travel properly between nerve cells in the brain. During a seizure the person may black out, his or her body may move involuntarily, and the eyes may roll. This usually lasts only for a few seconds or minutes, after which the brain cells go back to normal. The person may feel a little disoriented afterward, but rest usually helps him or her recover shortly.

Reducing the risk

If you have epilepsy, you can reduce the risk of seizures if you:

- avoid missing meals;
- make sure you get enough sleep;
- avoid illegal drugs, including marijuana;
- remember to take your medication;
- remember that alcohol could reduce your medication's effectiveness.

Some people have their first epileptic seizure around the time of puberty, probably because of the extra hormonal activity in their body. Often, people "grow out of it" by their late teens, although some will have seizures throughout their lives. If you have epilepsy, your doctor will prescribe medication that will help to reduce the number of seizures you experience.

Asthma

Asthma, a narrowing of the airways that makes breathing difficult, affects many children and teenagers. It can be mild or severe, and may be triggered by something to which you are sensitive or allergic. Common triggers are pets, dust, pollen, smoke, and exercise. If you have asthma, your doctor may suggest an inhaler, which enables medicine to reach your lungs quickly. It helps to relax the muscles around your airways so that you can breathe again.

Try to discover what triggers your asthma so that you can avoid those things. Keep your inhaler with you and don't be afraid to tell someone if you think you are having an attack. Many people find that asthma improves as they grow older.

Exercise
Vigorous exercise may bring on an asthma attack, so be prepared and always keep your inhaler with you.

Anemia

Anemia is caused by a lack of red blood cells and makes a person look pale and feel tired. Girls may become anemic during puberty because of the blood loss at menstruation. If your skin, gums, and the insides of your eyelids look pale and you feel more tired than usual, you could be anemic. Your doctor may prescribe iron supplements, but your condition could be improved by an iron-rich diet. Good sources of iron include liver, red meat, poultry, fish, eggs, nuts, dried fruits, peas, leafy green vegetables, and fortified cereals. Vitamin C helps your body to absorb the iron, so try to eat lots of fruit and vegetables that are rich in vitamin C.

Meningitis

Meningitis is an infection that causes inflammation of the meninges, the thin membranes surrounding the brain. Some forms are very serious and need urgent treatment with antibiotics. Others get better without treatment.

The serious forms, such as meningococcal meningitis, are spread by bacteria. Many people "carry" meningitis bacteria in the back of their throat, but they don't all develop the illness. Symptoms to watch for include fever, vomiting, severe headache, neck stiffness, aversion to bright light, joint pain, and drowsiness. There may be septicemia (blood poisoning) as well and this may cause a rash. If untreated, bacterial meningitis can kill within hours, so in suspected cases it is vital to get medical attention urgently.

"Six people in our school got meningitis last year. One of them was my best friend. It was really scary. I hadn't realized it could kill you."
(Vicki, age 14)

One in four teenagers carries meningitis bacteria, compared with one in 10 of the rest of the population. We don't know why this is, nor why some people develop meningitis and others don't. However, bacteria are spread by coughing, sneezing, and kissing. Since teenagers have lots of social interaction and close contact, they are at risk of infection.

Mononucleosis (mono)

Mononucleosis (also known as mono or "the kissing disease"), is an infectious disease which, like meningitis, tends to affect teenagers, especially students who work, socialize, and live closely together. It passes from person to person in saliva, so it can be spread through coughing, sneezing, or just in tiny droplets in the air when you talk. Symptoms include fever, sore throat and enlarged tonsils, tenderness in the abdominal area due to enlargement of the spleen, and painful swelling of the lymph glands, usually in the neck, armpits, or groin. These symptoms may be accompanied by extreme tiredness, headache, loss of appetite, and, occasionally, a rash. In most cases, the symptoms last less than a month. Doctors recommend rest, plenty of fluids, and a pain reliever to ease pain and reduce the fever. In a few people, the symptoms, especially the tiredness, can persist for longer, taking months to disappear completely.

While you have the illness you should avoid contact sports or any other risk of abdominal injury. This is because, if your spleen is enlarged, there is a risk of rupture, which causes internal bleeding and is a serious emergency.

"I think we take our health for granted. When I got mono last summer, it really wiped me out. I felt tired for months afterwards, and I really don't think my friends believed me."
(Nick, age 16)

The dangers of risky behavior

As you become more independent, you'll begin to find yourself in situations where you have to make decisions about risk and personal safety. Accidents tend to increase during the teenage years, resulting in traffic-related and sports-related injuries as well as injuries from accidents in the home. Poisoning also becomes more common, usually as a result of accidental overdose of drugs, including alcohol, prescription or "over the counter" medication, and "street" drugs.

Out of action
An accident can put you out of action for weeks.

Cigarettes, alcohol, and other "recreational" drugs

It is during puberty that some people try cigarettes, alcohol, and other drugs like marijuana or ecstasy. All of these are used "recreationally" because of their mind-altering effects. Some people begin to use these substances regularly, and some become dependent on them. The immediate effects of nicotine (in cigarettes), alcohol, and drugs may be to make you feel happy and confident or blissfully calm and worry-free, but all these substances also have harmful effects. Knowing about these can help you say "no" to using the substances.

Smoking is dangerous for anyone, but is particularly dangerous during puberty. Recent research in Canada has found that girls who start smoking within five years of starting their periods are 70 percent more likely than nonsmokers to develop breast cancer. Teenage smokers are also more likely than nonsmokers to suffer from asthma and other respiratory problems.

Alcohol can also affect young people very badly. It affects your reactions, coordination, memory, and judgment and it can make you sick. For adults there are guidelines on "safe levels" of drinking, but for young people, who come in all shapes and sizes and may not have finished developing, it is impossible to establish a "safe level." Tolerance to alcohol is often lower in teenagers than it is in adults.

Many drugs cause nausea, dizziness, depression, and anxiety, as well as making users feel paranoid or giving them terrifying hallucinations. The unpleasant effects of drugs can last for days. When someone's coordination and judgement are affected by alcohol or drugs, he or she is more likely to have an accident, become involved in a fight, or make a regrettable decision.

Inhalant abuse

Some young people try sniffing solvents like glue, or the gases from aerosols or cigarette lighters, to get mind-altering effects. This is called inhalant or volatile substance abuse (VSA) and is more dangerous than many people realize.

- VSA kills more teenagers than ecstasy, heroin, and cocaine put together.
- You can die the first (or any other) time you inhale.
- VSA kills one person every week.

I'm so ashamed

Sophie is 15 and recently, she went to a friend's party. "One of the guys smuggled in some Jack Daniels and stuff. I felt fine, so I just kept drinking. When I tried to go to the bathroom, I fell over and broke a mirror. Then I got dizzy and couldn't get up. Jade's parents came to see what was going on and I started shouting and swearing at them. Then I threw up. They called my dad to pick me up. The next morning, I felt so ill I thought I was dying, and I've never been so embarrassed in my life. I had to apologize to Jade's parents and I was grounded for three weeks."

Teenagers often say that smoking and drinking look cool and make them feel sophisticated. But coughing up phlegm, wheezing, and smelling like an ashtray aren't sophisticated. Nor are slurring your speech, falling over, and vomiting in public. Drugs can also affect appearance, making someone look pale and unhealthy and causing skin infections. They can make hair lank and eyes dull. You can often spot someone who sniffs solvents by the sores around his or her nose and mouth.

Long-term drug use can have a devastating effect on health. Smoking is a major cause of mouth and lung cancer, heart disease, and emphysema. Marijuana increases the risk of respiratory problems and may cause lung cancer. Alcohol also causes heart disease and damage to the stomach, liver, and brain. Cocaine can cause heart problems and damage to the lining of the nose, while taking ecstasy or using inhalants can damage the liver, kidneys, and brain. Injecting heroin can lead to gangrene, hepatitis, and AIDS.

Saying "no"

It's important to stand your ground if someone tries to make you do something you don't want to. The way you say "no" will affect their reaction. If you make an excuse, such as, "No, I've got to get home," the person will keep trying until you run out of excuses. If you're aggressive and shout "No, you're stupid and I'm going to tell your parents and everybody at school," you might end up in a fight. If you seem scared, the person may get a kick out of trying to make you join in. It's better to be calm, honest, and firm without being angry. Say, "No, thank you. It's really not my thing" or "It doesn't really appeal to me" each time and they'll soon see that there's no point in trying to persuade you. They may even respect you for this in the end.

Being yourself
Now that you are becoming an adult, you can make your own decisions. Don't be pressured. Do what you think is right.

You may even develop a crush on someone that you disliked before, such as the school bully. Crushes are a sort of practice run for real relationships. They are a focus for the sexual awareness that is caused by the hormonal activity you are experiencing. Usually, crushes are eventually replaced by a romantic interest in someone more attainable. However, most people continue to have and develop small crushes on people throughout their lives. Crushes are usually harmless—although being in love with someone who doesn't notice you or even know you exist can be difficult to handle. Occasionally, this can lead to someone who is usually very sensible behaving in a way that they later regret—pestering the person they have a crush on with phone calls, hanging around outside his or her house, or even following him or her. This sort of behavior is annoying for the person who is the object of the crush, and, later on, embarrassing for the person who has the crush. When you feel tempted to do any of those things, try and find a friend who will help you resist the urge.

Having a crush on an adult can be very confusing. Teens often believe that an adult returns their romantic feelings, when in fact, the adult is simply trying to be a good friend

Practice run
Having a crush is a powerful emotional experience, but it helps prepare you for romantic relationships you will have as an adult.

or teacher. A teenager who mistakenly believes an adult returns his or her feeling can cause many problems, including legal problems, for the object of his or her affection. It is also possible that an unethical adult or older teen may take advantage of an adolescent crush. They may try to get the person with the crush to do favors for them, or they may attempt to initiate a physical relationship with the teenager. It is wonderful to have friends of all different ages, but if you ever feel that an adult or older teen is trying to take advantage of you, you should speak to your parents or a school counselor about it.

"At first, it was sweet that my sister's best friend liked me, but then she started hanging around outside the garage where I work, e-mailing me, and calling my house. I had to ask her parents to make her stop."
(Andrew, age 19)

If you spend too much time "mooning" over a crush, your parents or a teacher may become concerned about you and encourage you to develop other interests. They may say things that hurt your feelings unintentionally, or cause you to feel that they are making fun of you. Although you may not appreciate the way they give advice, you should try to listen to them.

Seeing the danger

"When I was 14, I used to babysit for Lynne and Billy. Billy was about 30, but I really liked him. Looking back, I suppose I did flirt with him. I dressed up to go over there, and tried to make myself look older. Lynne used to take me home, but then Billy started driving me. It was great to have him to myself. He talked and told me jokes. Then one night he stopped the car away from my house and tried to kiss me. It was what I'd wanted, but when it happened it was really scary. I pulled away and said I had to get back or my parents would be looking for me. He looked annoyed at first, and then laughed. I didn't babysit for them again. Lynne said she didn't think it was working out, and I was glad. My younger sister's 14 now and, if I think of some guy of 30 trying to kiss her, I can see it's weird. It's strange how you don't see the danger when it's you."
(Anna, age 16)

Ben's crush on Rory

Ben is 14 and is worried about his feelings towards his older brother's best friend, Rory. "Rory's 19 and he's been coming to our house for years. He used to treat me like a little kid. But lately he's been really talking to me, asking me about school and stuff. I've always liked him, but now I feel as if I'm in love with him or something. The other day, he sat right next to me on the couch and my heart was beating so loud that I thought he would hear it. I used to think about girls, but now I can't stop thinking about Rory. Does this mean I'm gay?"

The fact that Ben feels affectionate toward Rory in the story above is not unusual in the circumstances. Rory is someone he knows well, likes, and trusts. What is more, he is now treating Ben like an adult, which is flattering. Ben's hormones are making him sexually aware, so it's normal for him to focus his attention on someone. He says that he used to think about girls—but maybe there aren't

Homophobia

Homophobia is being afraid of, disliking, or discriminating against homosexuals.

Homophobia can be acted out in a variety of ways. Some people use the words "gay," "queer," or "dike" in hateful ways. Others pick on or bully people they believe to be gay. In some cases, innocent people have been brutally beaten or killed because they were thought to be gay. Many of the victims of homophobia are teenagers.

Adolescence is a difficult time and it can make people uncomfortable with those who seem different from them. Some people bully others because they are scared that if they don't, they themselves will be thought of as gay.

It can be difficult not to join in if your friends display homophobic attitudes. Remember, though, that the person you are picking on is also going through a rough time, and by your actions you are making his or her adolescence worse. If you are a victim of such behavior, talk to an adult you can trust.

many girls around at the moment, so he is focusing on Rory. He might be gay and he might not. Being attracted to Rory is not enough to make it clear.

In time, Ben's feelings for Rory (or for other boys or men) may change, disappear, or get stronger. Many people believe that your sexuality is set or "programmed" into your genetic makeup, developing gradually through your teens. During puberty, it is quite normal and not particularly unusual to have sexual feelings for people of both sexes.

First love

As time goes on, you will move from crushes and romantic and sexual fantasies into wanting a real relationship and actual physical contact.

Your first experience of romantic love can be magical. You may have a warm, floaty feeling inside and spend hours just thinking about him or her. It can also be confusing and upsetting. You are having certain feelings for the first time, and you may not be sure how to handle them.

First love
When two people begin to go out as a couple, any physical contact—for example, holding hands or an arm around the waist or shoulders—is exciting.

When you're in love, it's natural to want to kiss and touch each other. This is part of the closeness and intimacy that develop in romantic relationships. At first, a couple may hold hands and sit close together. Later on they might move to more intimate touching.

But while kissing and touching can be an exciting way to satisfy the intense feelings you may experience, you need to be aware that very intimate touching (where the male and female genitals come into contact) carries a risk of pregnancy.

Waiting for a happy sex life

The changes that happen to your body during puberty make you physically mature enough to have sex, and you may sometimes feel very much that you want to. But teenagers are not mature enough to handle the emotional responsibility and consequences of having sex.

Myth

You can only get pregnant if you have sex and the man ejaculates inside the woman's vagina.

Fact

Semen may leak from the penis during sexual excitement. If the penis is near the entrance of the vagina, semen can enter and a pregnancy may result.

He wants to go all the way

"I'd liked Brett for ages, so I couldn't believe it when he asked me out. I really, really like him, but he wants to go all the way with me, and I'm not sure I want to. He said I must be frigid because, if I really liked him, I'd want to have sex with him. I'm still not sure, but I'm scared he'll break up with me if I don't."
(Charlene, age 15)

In the story above, Charlene is right to be cautious. Having sex for the first time is a very big step and one that should not be taken lightly. She knows she isn't ready yet, and Brett's behavior amounts to blackmail. Even if she did feel ready, Brett clearly does not respect her, or he wouldn't put pressure on her to do something she is unsure of. No one should ever say "yes" unless he or she has thought it through seriously and is absolutely certain. It may sound weird, but you might want to consider talking to your parents before deciding whether or not to have sex. Your parents were young once, too and they may have helpful advice for you.

You need to understand the implications, not only the physical risk of pregnancy or sexually transmitted disease, but also the effect that having sex may have on your relationship and on how you feel about yourself. Above all, it's your choice. You shouldn't rush into having sex because your partner or your best friend thinks you should, because your friends say "everybody else has," or because you're a certain age. Having sex for the wrong reasons can be disappointing and leave you feeling miserable. Afterward you may have doubts about whether that person was really special enough for you to share your body with, or whether you had really wanted to wait.

"Jo and I got carried away and ended up having sex without a condom. Later, we were both pretty upset and worried. Eventually we broke up because of it. I wish we hadn't done it "
(Tom, age 16)

Remember that there is nothing wrong with waiting. Many people choose to wait until they are married. If you begin a sexual relationship at the right time and after careful thought, sex can be a wonderful, intimate form of communication between two people who love and respect each other. You probably have 70 or more years ahead of you during which you can enjoy sex with someone really special, so there's no need to rush.

Having fun as a group

Having friends of both sexes is important and will enrich all your relationships.

Sexual abuse

Usually, developing into a sexually mature adult is an exciting experience, even if it can be a little unsettling. Unfortunately, for some people, it can be a very unhappy time. Occasionally, a young person becomes the victim of sexual abuse at around the time of puberty. If an adult engages in sexual activity with a young person, even without violence, it is sexual abuse.

Sometimes someone who has been sexually abused as a child only realizes the meaning of what has been happening when he or she reaches puberty and understands more about sexual activity. Up until then, he or she may not have recognized that the contact with the abuser has been inappropriate, especially if, as is often the case, it is a family member or friend—someone loved and trusted. The abuser may have convinced the child that they are playing a special, secret game. Some abusers threaten their victims—for instance, "If you tell anyone, I'll kill your mom." It is only when the child begins to mature that he or she sees that this is just a threat to keep him or her quiet.

Rape and sexual assault

If someone touches you or makes you touch them in a sexual way without your consent, it is sexual assault. Rape is when someone is sexually penetrated without his or her consent. Rape may happen as part of a pattern of sexual abuse or just once, either by someone the victim knows or by a stranger.

Fact

Although it's more common for sexual violence to be committed by men and boys against girls and women, this is not always the case. Women can carry out sexual assaults, and boys and men can be raped.

Your body is your own and no one should touch it in a way you don't like, even if you have had or are having a relationship with the person. "Date rape"—where there is or has been a relationship between the rapist and the person raped—can be just as devastating as rape by a stranger. Some people don't report it because the rapist tells them it's their fault for leading the rapist on. Even if you have agreed to have sex with someone in the past, it is still rape if you do not agree to have sex at this time.

Rape, sexual assault, and sexual abuse are always the fault of the person who carries out the attack. They are never the fault of the person they have happened to. However, there are common-sense precautions that girls should take. For example, girls should not walk alone in unfamiliar areas. Girls should also not agree to go to an empty house or deserted location with someone they do not know well. Girls should not drink alcohol or take drugs around boys they do not know well and trust.

If you have ever been abused, assaulted, or raped, it may help to talk to someone about what happened. If it's difficult to talk to your family, try your doctor or perhaps a trusted teacher. You could also call your local rape crisis center and speak to someone anonymously.

Talking it through
Some counselors are specially trained to support people who have suffered from a sexual crime.

Drug-assisted rape

This is the practice of spiking a drink with drugs to alter a person's awareness and behavior so that they will put up no resistance to rape. Many of the "rape drugs" used are easy-to-obtain prescription drugs and they are most commonly slipped into alcoholic drinks but also into tea, coffee, hot chocolate, or soft drinks. There may be a slight change in the taste, but it can be difficult to spot.

To reduce the risk of anyone spiking your drink, never leave your drink unattended, never accept a drink from someone you don't trust completely, and do not continue your drink if it looks or tastes different. If you suddenly feel very drunk after only one or two drinks, get help from someone you are sure you can trust and get to a safe place immediately.

4 Changing Relationships
Emotional Development

The word "relationships" may make you think first of a romantic and/or physical relationship, especially if you are just starting to experience this kind. But it's important to remember that the relationships you already have—with friends, parents, brothers, and sisters—will also be changing. Often they develop into satisfying adult relationships fairly easily. But sometimes unfamiliar emotions and the natural desire to become an independent adult in your own right can cause problems. It may be that you find these new feelings difficult to cope with, or it may be that your friends and family have difficulty accepting the "new you."

"Tara used to be my best friend, but then she started hanging out with this boy in our class, and now he's all she ever talks about. She's getting really boring."
(Charlotte, age 14)

Friends

As your outlook on life and general interests change, your group of friends may change, too. People you thought were great may now seem boring or childish, and someone you hardly ever talked

Sharing views
Some of the friends you make now may be friends for life.

to is interested now in the same things as you. All of this changing is normal. Adulthood means you start to become more of an individual, refining your interests and opinions and choosing friends that "fit" with these.

You may keep one or two close friends, or you may stop seeing them for awhile and become friendly again later. This often happens when people are developing at different rates—you want to talk about politics, and your less mature friend wants to play Spiderman. It can be unsettling, but gradually you will make new friends and existing ones will "catch up."

Siblings

Brothers and sisters can be your best friends or your worst enemies, at least for some of the time. Maturity may help you to overcome your differences as you make a conscious effort to get along. Or you may find you fight even more, especially with younger siblings. As you get older, you will naturally want more privacy. This can be difficult if you share a room with an eight-year-old. You may have been used to sharing the same friends, all playing together as one big group. Your kid brother or sister will still want to join in, but you may want to keep your friends to yourself, talking about things that the younger ones wouldn't understand.

The best way through this difficult time is to try to remember that things will improve. Your younger sibling may be determined to annoy you. But it's probably only because he or she is feeling left behind. Don't worry; he or she will be growing up soon, too. If siblings cause real

Pulling apart
Younger brothers and sisters can get on your nerves, but in a few years they will be feeling as you do now.

problems—never allowing you any privacy for example, or stealing your clothes, makeup, or CDs—take time to talk to them. Perhaps you could let them into your world, just a little, on the understanding that they respect your right to your own space and friends. It's amazing what you can achieve by letting them have a dab of your after-shave or a smear of your lipstick. If this doesn't work, you may have to ask your parents for help. There could be an easy solution, like having your brother or sister go out when you have friends over.

Parents

Talking to your parents can be difficult because you tend to assume they won't understand—but they may surprise you. If you explain what's wrong rather than just complain about it, they might prove more supportive than you expected. Parents often don't notice their children growing up, possibly because it's something they find difficult. When you were little, they were the center of your world. These days, you are more interested in other things and other people. Parents can be scared that they are losing you, especially when they see that you don't need them as much as you used to. This can make them reluctant to let you do things, even when they don't mean to be tough on you.

"I remember what we did when we were 15—lying about our age to get into bars. One of my friends fell off a motorcycle and broke his collar bone. I shudder to think about it now."
(David, dad)

Mostly, when parents get stressed, it's because they are worried. They know, even if they don't want to accept, that you are becoming an independent adult. You want to experience adult things, to take risks and to learn about adult life. Your parents want this for you, too, but they don't want you to get hurt. Most parents also say that they worry because they remember things they did at your age. Try to get them to talk about this—it might help you both to see the other side of things.

"So many bad things can happen to youngsters these days. Harriet thinks I want to stop her from having fun, but it's just that I look at my beautiful daughter and couldn't stand to see her hurt."
(Maggie, mom)

Hannah wants to stay out late

"I'll be 16 in three weeks. I've just had this huge fight with my mom over the time I come in. I think I should be allowed to stay out until midnight once I'm 16. After all, I'm legally old enough to get married. She thinks I should come in at 10:30 PM 'and not a minute later.' I'm sick of being treated like a kid. I'm going to a party next week and it'll be SO embarrassing if I have to leave early. I might just stay late anyway. She can't stop me."
(Hannah)

In the case of Hannah above, neither she nor her mom can see the other's point of view. They won't find a solution unless they are prepared to compromise. Hannah could suggest that, now that she is a little older, her curfew could be extended to 11:30 on weekends. If she is going somewhere special, perhaps she could stay out until midnight, as long as she agrees to let her mom or dad pick her up. If she goes to her mom with this suggestion, she will show that she is able to think in an adult way. If she sticks to the agreement, her mom will know she can be trusted and may well allow her to stay out even later. If her mom doesn't agree to this, Hannah could very calmly try to find out what concerns her mother has. At the moment, Hannah's mom may think she isn't mature enough to be trusted. Claiming that she's old enough to get married and threatening to stay out anyway will not convince her parents that she is being sensible.

Body piercing

Today this can be an area of conflict between parents and teenagers. Piercing is a relatively new fad and so your parents may think only "bad" or "weird" kids have piercings. They'll also argue (rightly) that piercings can be dangerous. From your point of view, a piercing would be cool, and choosing how you look is a way of expressing your individuality. This can be difficult for parents, since it is yet further evidence that you are growing up and making your own choices.

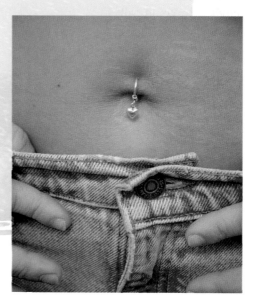

If you are thinking of having a piercing, you should be aware of the risks. Piercings can become infected, causing serious illness or even death. There's also a risk of hemorrhage (severe bleeding from a blood vessel being pierced), especially with tongue piercings. If your parents agree to let you get a piercing, choose a safe, licenced piercing salon.

You may also argue with your parents about the way you dress, how you wear your hair, the music you listen to, and the friends you hang out with. It's all part of the same conflict: You are becoming an individual and you want to express this by exercising your right to choose your own style, music, and friends. Your parents may resist at first, but they will get used to it, especially if you don't shock them too much.

"My mom used to yell at me all the time about the state of my room. But now we have a deal. I promise to bring out dirty laundry and cups, plates, and stuff, and she lets me keep my room as I want." (Rea, age 14)

Feeling under pressure

Pressure can come from many directions. Parents can put pressure on you, often without meaning to. They want you to do well at school, to be great at sports, and to be the most popular kid in the area. If you feel pressured by your parents, try explaining that you are finding it difficult to cope. They won't know you are unhappy if you don't tell them. If there is extra pressure because of exams or schoolwork, maybe they could help you work out a homework or study schedule. Or maybe you could temporarily give up one of your after-school activities. If you are struggling with schoolwork, tell your teachers. They want you to do well and may be able to juggle your schedule to help you through any difficulties. If you can't talk to your parents, perhaps an older brother or sister could help, or maybe you could talk to your grandparents—they may be less busy than your parents and often have more time to help you organize your life.

The fact that you and your friends are developing at different rates can cause conflict among you. If all your friends are dating, for example, you could be made to feel that you're weird if you are not interested in dating yet. Peer pressure is often given as a reason for people starting to smoke, drink, or take drugs, having piercings, or even bullying someone. Try to be strong and trust your instincts—if something feels wrong, don't do it.

Feeling out of step

Teenagers all develop at different rates. This can mean that you no longer have much in common with some of your friends.

A mind of your own

"I get fed up with the idea that if one person does something, everyone else has to do it, too. I was out with some friends the other night and someone had a cigarette. They passed it around and kept telling me to try it. I said I didn't want to—it costs too much and it kills you. Then this girl called me 'chicken.' I said I'd rather be a live chicken than a dead sheep, and everyone laughed, so it was fine. Sometimes it's not that easy, though. I think if someone tries to make you do something you don't want to, you should just say, 'Thanks, but no thanks.' Or if they're not saying anything but they're making you feel bad for not joining in, just find something more interesting to do. They'll soon see that you've got a mind of your own."
(Shanna, age 14)

Young love

When you start to develop romantic relationships, adults may not take you seriously, saying that you are too young to be in love or that "puppy love" doesn't last. This can be upsetting. It may well be that it doesn't last, but that does not mean that it isn't love. It is a real and strong emotion that can make you feel great or, when a relationship goes wrong, terrible. Sometimes first love lasts for months or years; sometimes it's over in a week.

Being in love can be painful, for instance, when the person you love doesn't love you back. You cannot make someone love you. Sometimes, it helps to fill your time with other activities—going out with friends, or whatever you enjoy. Taking your mind off the situation won't make you stop loving the person, but it gives your heart some recovery time. Then one day, you'll think about him or her and find that it doesn't hurt any more.

When a relationship ends, there are a lot of emotions to deal with. If you still love the person, there's the pain of missing him or her and knowing that your love is not returned. This can be almost physical, like an empty ache in your stomach. You may feel angry, especially if you feel you have been treated badly. You may also feel a sense of grief that the relationship is over, even if it was not very happy at the end. All these feelings are normal, and we all experience them at least once in our lives. It may not seem possible at the moment, but you will get over it. In the meantime, take each day as it comes and try to enjoy the things you still have. Talk to close friends about how you feel, and try to laugh at least once a day, even if you cry as

Emotional rollercoaster: the highs ...

The hormone activity that brings about the physical changes of puberty also affects your emotions. You may find that your mood varies from day to day or even from hour to hour, swinging from elation to misery and back again.

well. Laughing releases chemicals in the brain that help you to feel good, so it really is worth trying.

You may find yourself in a relationship that is not making you happy, although the other person wants it to continue. When you are used to being part of a couple, making the decision to be on your own is not easy. Telling somone that it is over is difficult, too. Try to resist the temptation to get somebody else to do this for you. E-mails make it easier to make hurtful remarks, especially if we tend to press "send" without rereading and considering what we've said. If you really can't do it face to face or on the phone, a handwritten letter is probably the best option. The first few days after you end a relationship are the worst. Don't be tempted to get back together because someone makes you feel guilty.

"It was hard telling Kim that I didn't want to go out with her any more. I still liked her and didn't want to hurt her."
(Mike, age 15)

Depression

Considering how much there is to cope with during puberty, it's not surprising that some teenagers become depressed. Young people in the 21st century may have a worse time than in the past, because marriages and other family relationships break down more frequently, leaving children and teenagers in unstable situations. When they experience trauma, such as relationship problems or exam stress, they may feel isolated and unable to cope with their lives.

... and lows
The breakup of a relationship is just one of the traumatic events in a young person's life that can cause depression.

Mild feelings of depression—feeling sad and tearful for a few days—are common and usually pass quickly. Severe depression, where everything looks bleak and life does not seem worth living, needs professional attention. If you think you might be depressed, see your doctor or ask your parents to arrange this for you. The doctor may suggest antidepressants and counseling. In the meantime, avoid alcohol since it can make depression worse, get plenty of exercise, and try to remember that the awful feeling will not last forever.

Signs of depression

- lack of energy
- irritability
- anxiety
- tearfulness
- poor concentration
- changes in eating or sleeping patterns
- loss of interest in school, friends, appearance, interests
- feeling suicidal

Self-harm and suicide

Self-harm—where someone deliberately damages his or her body—often begins in the later stages of puberty. It is not known why teenagers harm themselves. It may be that the physical and emotional changes that are taking place make them feel they have no control over their bodies, and little control over their lives. Harming themselves gives them a sense of taking control. If the person has low self-esteem, perhaps due to bullying or physical or sexual abuse, their self-harm may be a way of subconsciously punishing themselves. It may also be a way of trying to let their parents know that they are hurting inside, or even of punishing their parents for the way they feel.

Tragically, suicide among teenagers is not uncommon. According to a study done in 2000, half of all young people know someone who has contemplated, attempted, or committed suicide. Like self-harm, suicide is often the result of a combination of factors, usually but not always including depression. Young people who have been abused have an increased risk of self-harm and suicide. If someone says he or she feels suicidal, the warning should always be taken seriously.

CHAPTER 4

A learning period

Puberty can be a difficult time. Sometimes it may seem that everything is wrong—your moods go up and down, you're always arguing with your family, you can't get the person you dream about to notice you and when you look in the mirror, you don't even look like you any more.

In the space of just a few years, you will change from a child into an adult, which means that you are dealing with far more than just physical changes. You are managing many things that, until now, your parents dealt with on your behalf. This can mean that you get to have more fun, but the new responsibility may be daunting, so teenagers often find this time difficult to cope with.

Puberty is, in part, a learning period in which you practice the skills that you'll need in adult life: for example, forming relationships, making choices about how you look, whom you choose as your friends, and what sort of things you want to do in the future. At the same time, you may be battling with people who find it hard to accept that you're growing up. Try to remember that we all go through it, and it won't last forever. Keep reminding yourself that you're well on the way to becoming an independent adult, living life the way you choose.

In it together
Everyone goes through puberty. It may be tough, but you will soon be adults, enjoying your freedom and independence.

Glossary

AIDS acquired immunodeficiency syndrome, the end result of infection with HIV, the human immunodeficiency virus. The virus weakens the immune system, leaving the victim increasingly unable to resist various infections and tumors.

anorexia nervosa eating disorder in which a person deliberately keeps his or her weight below a healthy level by not eating enough

antibiotic medicine that kills bacteria

antiperspirant cosmetic preparation that reduces the amount of sweat produced. It may be combined with a deodorant, making an antiperspirant deodorant.

bacteria single-cell organisms in the body that can cause disease

calorie unit of energy. The number of calories in food is a measurement of the amount of energy that food gives

circulation movement of blood around the body

clitoris small, sensitive organ that is part of the female genitals. Its only known function is sexual pleasure.

contraception avoiding conception (the start of a pregnancy)

cyst swelling within a tissue, often containing fluid. It is not a cancer.

deodorant cosmetic preparation that neutralizes body odor by controlling the growth of bacteria

electron micrograph image obtained using an electron microscope, a powerful instrument that gives extremely high magnification. Sometimes colors are put in by computer to highlight particular features.

emphysema lung damage that makes breathing painful and difficult

fertile physically capable of becoming pregnant, if you are a girl; or physically capable of making someone pregnant, if you are a boy

fertilization joining of the male and female gametes (sperm and ovum) from which a baby grows

follicle a small sac or cavity

gangrene decay of flesh tissue and death of part of the body, due to loss of blood supply

genitals the external sex organs: in men, the testicles and penis; in women, the vulva and clitoris

hepatitis inflammation of the liver due to a viral infection or the presence of toxins (for example, as a result of alcohol abuse)

hormone chemical messenger produced in a gland in the body

inflammation response of body tissues to injury or infection, usually resulting in pain, redness, heat, and swelling

iron supplement	medicine that provides extra iron. People who are anemic require extra iron, as do pregnant women.	**sexually active**	taking part in physical sexual relationships
mucus	slimy substance created by the mucous membranes as a protective lubricant. Infection may cause increased production of mucus.	**sexually transmitted disease (STD)**	infection that can only be caught by sexual contact. Chlamydia and gonorrhea are two examples.
obesity	excess fat in the body, caused by eating more food than is necessary for the body's energy requirements	**spleen**	organ situated behind the stomach, responsible for the filtration of the blood, production of white blood cells, and removal of old red blood cells
paranoid	having unfounded feelings of persecution	**thyroid gland**	gland situated at the front of the neck, responsible for producing metabolism-regulating hormones
pelvic inflammation	infection of the female reproductive organs	**uterus**	hollow female organ where a baby grows, also known as the womb
pelvis	basin-shaped area of bone in the lower body. It helps to protect parts of the digestive and urinary systems. In females it also houses nearly all the reproductive organs.	**vulva**	area around the vaginal opening
pituitary gland	pea-sized, hormone-secreting gland in the brain		
rectum	end of the digestive tract, just inside the anus		
respiratory	concerned with respiration, the process of breathing		
scrotum	the sac that contains the testicles		

Resources

Organizations

Al-Anon/Alateen
Al-Anon is a support group for the families and friends of alcoholics. Alateen is a support group for young people with an addiction to alcohol.
www.al-anon.alateen.org
(888) 425-2666

Lyric
Lyric is a support center for gay, lesbian, bisexual, and transgendered youth.
www.lyric.org

Help Lines and Websites

National Runaway Switchboard
www.nrscrisisline.org
(800) 621-4000

Rape, Abuse, and Incest National Network
(800) 656-4673

www.goaskalice.columbia.edu/index.html
This site gives honest medical advice on a variety of subjects for teenagers.

www.teenadviceonline.org
This site features information and advice about a variety of teen issues.

Books

Blackstone, Margaret. *Girl Stuff: A Survival Guide to Growing Up.* New York: Harcourt Children's Books, 2000.

Bryan, Jenny. *Health and Fitness: Adolescence.* Chicago: Raintree, 2000.

Mostache, Harriet S., and Karen Unger, Mike Gordon (illustrator). *Too Old for This, Too Young for That!: Your Survival Guide for the Middle-School Years.* Minneapolis: Free Spirit Publishing, 2000.

Winkler, Kathleen. *Teens, Depression and the Blues.* Berkeley Heights, N.J.: Enslow, 2000.

Index